W9-BBO-017

¡HOLA!
Let's Learn Spanish
Visit New Places and Make New Friends!

by Judy Martialay

PoliglotKidz Press

To Ruthie and her generation.
May you love languages.

PoliglotKidz Press, Sea Cliff, N.Y.
ISBN 978-0-9911324-0-9 (softcover edition)
Text and illustrations copyright © 2015 by Judy Martialay
Editor: Susan Korman
Library of Congress Control Number: 2015948565

For audio, please go to http://polyglotkidz.com

CONTENTS

¡HOLA!

Hello, children. **¡Hola, niños!** My name is Pete the Pilot. My job is to fly kids around the world. When I stop in different countries, I visit places and learn about life in those countries. I meet the people. I also try to learn their language. People really like this, and I make friends this way.

Today we're going to Mexico. You're going to discover that Mexicans do a lot of the same things as we do here. For example, Mexican kids love to play games. They play many of the same games that you play. But part of the fun of traveling around the world is seeing how folks do things differently!

Let's learn more about Mexican children. Let's begin by learning their language, Spanish.

Below are some words that are very useful. You will have time to study these words during the plane trip to Mexico. Bring clothes for warm weather, because we are going to land in a sunny bean field **¡en un campo de frijoles!**

Fasten your safety belts. We're ready to leave for Mexico!

Hello **Hola**
My name is…(Pete). **Me llamo …(Pedro).**
How are you? **¿Qué tal?**
Very well **Muy bien**
And you? **¿Y tú?**
Please **Por favor**
Thank you **Gracias**
Yes **Sí**
No **No**
Good-bye **Adiós**
one **uno**
two **dos**
three **tres**
four **cuatro**
five **cinco**

PANCHITO

Cri ...Cri...Cri say the crickets. They are chirping under the hot sun that is shining down on the bean field. The beans **los frijoles** are growing in their rows of plants. Nothing is moving. Look! **¡Miren!** Something *is* moving. It's jumping! In fact, it's jumping towards us!

"Hola, niños. Me llamo Panchito, the Mexican jumping bean. Look at how high I can jump. **¡Miren!"**

Panchito jumps around the field. He wants to talk to **los frijoles**.

"**¡Hola! ¿Qué tal?**" says Panchito.

But **los frijoles** don't answer. They don't talk or play. They are not jumping beans like Panchito. They just stay in one place and grow.

It's lonely here in the bean field with no friends to play with.

Nearby, Mr. Villa, **el señor Villa**, the owner of the farm, is looking at his **frijoles.** He counts the rows of beans: "**Uno, dos, tres, cuatro, cinco.** Five rows make five huge baskets! **Muy bien**. I'll make a lot of money when I sell these beans." He calls to some workers, "Let's pick the beans and put them in the baskets. Let's go, men! **¡Vamos, hombres!**" Panchito doesn't want to be left out, so he jumps into a basket full of beans.

El señor Villa puts the baskets of beans in the truck.

"Where are we going? What's going on? **¿Qué pasa?**"
Panchito asks.

Los frijoles don't answer. They don't really care.

The truck bumps along the road, past fields and over hills.

El señor Villa is headed towards the village. He is taking the beans to the market **el mercado,** where he will sell them.

At **el mercado**, vendors call out their wares, "Hats, tomatoes, beans! **¡Sombreros, tomates, frijoles!** Everything very cheap!"

There are stands for fruit, vegetables, clothing, and blankets. Panchito and **los frijoles** are in a pile at the bean stand.

Mrs. Gomez **la señora Gómez** comes along and looks at the beans. "Delicious **Riquísimo**," says **la señora Gómez** to the vendor. "I can't wait to make a delicious dish of beans for my family... a bag of **frijoles**, **por favor**."

"Gosh **¡Caramba!**" says Panchito. "I don't want to end up in a dish of **frijoles** with the other beans. They don't care, but I do! Oh, how awful! **¡Ay!¡Qué horror!**"

The vendor starts to scoop up **los frijoles** to put them in a bag. Panchito is so frightened that he takes a huge leap, and he lands in a pile of candy **caramelos** at the candy stand.

A few minutes later, **la señora Moreno** comes along and buys the pile of **caramelos** with Panchito hiding inside. She takes **los caramelos** home, and puts them inside **una piñata**. **La piñata** is in the shape of a donkey and has bright colors. Tomorrow is Magdalena's birthday party. The children will break **la piñata** and eat **los caramelos** that fall out.

At the party **la fiesta**, **la piñata** is hung above the children.
"I can't see," says Roberto. "I'm blindfolded. How am I going
to hit **la piñata**?"

"You have to be blindfolded. That's the rule," explains **la
señora Moreno**. "Here's a stick. Try to break **la piñata** with
it. When **la piñata** is broken, **los caramelos** will fall out.
We'll give you hints."

Roberto starts swinging with his stick.

"Higher, not lower! Not here, there!" The other children sing
and shout to Roberto. "Hit it, Roberto!"

Roberto keeps missing, so soon it's someone else's turn.

Finally, **la piñata** breaks open. Out come **los caramelos**, and out jumps Panchito!

As the children run to pick up **los caramelos**, Magdalena sees something moving. "What is that?"

"**¡Un insecto! ¡Ay! ¡Qué horror!**" the children cry.

"He's *not* an insect," Magdalena says, "**¡Miren!** A jumping bean!"

"**¡Un saltarín!** How cute! **¡Qué mono!** "

Magdalena rushes to pick up Panchito in the palm of her hand.

"**Hola,**" says Panchito.

"**Hola, señor Saltarín.** What's your name? **¿Cómo te llamas?**"

"**Me llamo Panchito**."

The other children run over to look. "**¡Qué mono!**" The children take turns holding Panchito.

"Where am I?" asks Panchito. The last thing that he remembers is being in a pile of **caramelos.**

"You're at our party in our house," explains Magdalena.

"You've come to just the right place. You are the best surprise of the party! Welcome! **¡Bienvenido!**"

"Dad! **¡Papá!** Mom! **¡Mamá!** Come to meet Panchito, **un saltarín**! He just fell out of **la piñata!** What a surprise! **¡Qué sorpresa!**"

Panchito is happy too. He has found the friends **los amigos** that he was looking for, and he has found a new home.

Panchito can't wait to play. He has an idea. "Let's play hide and seek. I'll go hide."

"Oh, no, Panchito. You're so little, we would never find you."

"What else can we play?"

"Let's jump rope."

"I'm a *jumping* bean. I can jump so high that you won't even see me!"

"We can play lots of games. But first let's eat some **caramelos** from **la piñata.**"

"**¡Vamos, amigos!**"

TE TOCA A TI: *It's Your Turn*

¡ Hola!

Here's how Panchito introduces himself:
¡Hola! Me llamo Panchito. *Hello, my name is Panchito.*

¿Y tú? *And you?* **¿Cómo te llamas?** *What's your name?*

Now it's your turn:
¡Hola! Me llamo (your name).

Introduce yourself in Spanish to everyone you see!

¿Qué tal?

When Panchito wants to know how the other beans are, he asks: **¿Qué tal?**
If they could talk, here's what they would answer:

muy bien   **bien**   **así así**   **mal**

¿Qué tal?   **¡Mal!**

Now, ask your friends and family **¿Qué tal?**

Cosas *Things*

*Here are some new words. Can you guess what they mean?**

 un globo   **un pastel**   **un regalo**   **un libro**

What would you like to have for your **fiesta de cumpleaños** *birthday party?*

una piñata   un sombrero   un globo   tomates   caramelos
        un regalo   un libro   frijoles   un pastel

¿Dónde? *Where?*

¿Dónde hay....? *Where is there...?*
Where can you find these people and things?

en casa *at home*   **en un campo** *in a field*   **en la escuela** *at school*

un amigo
un sombrero
tomates
un libro
un caramelo
un insecto
niños
frijoles
un hombre
un saltarín

left to right: a balloon, a cake, a gift, a book

Búsqueda del tesoro *Treasure Hunt*

En casa *At home*

Explore your home inside and out, front and back. Can you find these people and things?
¿Sí o no?

un sombrero
tres caramelos
un tomate
frijoles
un libro
una señora
un pastel
dos hombres
un amigo
una piñata
un insecto
un campo
un globo

En el supermercado *At the Supermarket*

*Look around **el supermercado** or imagine that you are at **el supermercado**. Can you find these people and things?* **¿Sí o no?**

caramelos
tomates
pasteles
hombres
globos
sombreros
frijoles
regalos

Expresión diaria *Daily Expression*

*Here's an expression for each day of the week. Try to use each expression several times during each day. Mark how many times you used that expression in the chart below. For example, if you use ¿**Qué tal?** three times on **lunes**, Monday, write the number 3.*

¿Qué tal?

¡Riquísimo!

¡Qué mono! *

¡Caramba!

¡Qué horror!

¡Qué sorpresa!

¿Qué pasa ?

Mi Semana	
My Week	
Lunes Monday	
martes Tuesday	
miércoles Wednesday	
jueves Thursday	
viernes Friday	
sábado Saturday	
domingo Sunday	

*(When talking to, or about, females, use ¡**Qué mona! Mono/a** can mean "cute" or "pretty.")

un pájaro

¿Dónde está Panchito? *Where is Panchito?*

Have fun acting out this skit with one or more people. Panchito and friends start by bragging about what they can do.

Amigo*1: Yo* canto bien.	I sing well. *(Sing.)*
Amigo 2: Yo juego al béisbol.	I play baseball. *(Swing a bat.)*
Amigo 3: Yo bailo bien.	I dance well. *(Dance.)*
Amigo 4: Yo corro.	I run. *(Run.)*
Panchito: Yo salto... y salto...	I jump *(jump),* and jump *(jump*
y salto...	*higher)* and jump *(jump higher).*
¡Ay!	Oh! *(Shout, with voice fading out, and disappear.)*
Pájaro: Pío, pío	*(Bird:)* Chirp, Chirp *(Fly by.)*
Amigos: ¿Qué pasa?	What's going on?
¿Dónde está Panchito?	Where is Panchito?*(Look up, down, around.)*
Amigo 1: ¿En el jardín?	In the garden?
Amigo 2: ¿En casa?	In the house?
Amigo 3: ¿En un armario?	In a closet?
Amigo 4: ¿En un árbol?	In a tree?
Amigos: ¿En un plato de frijoles?	On a dish of frijoles? *(Look horrified.)*
¡Qué horror!	That's awful!
¡Socorro!	Help! *(Run around looking for help.)*
Panchito: Hola, amigos. Aquí estoy.	Hi, friends. Here I am.*(Appear, looking upset.)*
Amigos: ¿Qué pasó, Panchito?	What happened, Panchito?
Panchito: Un pájaro me cogió en	A bird caught me in its beak.
su pico.	
Amigos: ¡Qué miedo!	That's scary!
Panchito: Pero me soltó.	But it dropped me.
Todos: ¡Qué suerte!	*(All)* That's lucky! *(Everyone says together.)*

un armario

---

amigo/amiga: *In the skit,* **amigo** *stands for a boy* **amigo** *or girl* **amiga** *who is a friend.*
yo *When saying "I+verb"* **yo** *isn't necessary because the verb ending in* **-o,** *or another ending, expresses I. It is used here for emphasis because the children are bragging.*

RINCÓN CULTURAL
Culture Corner

El español: Spanish is spoken in many countries and regions. Can you name some of these places? (*See answers at bottom of page.*)

México: Mexico is in North America. It is south of the United States and north of Guatemala. Can you find Mexico on a map of the world?

Spanish is spoken in Argentina, Bolivia, Chile, Colombia, Costa Rica, Cuba, Dominican Republic, Ecuador, Equatorial Guinea, El Salvador, Guatemala, Honduras, Mexico, Nicaragua, Panama, Paraguay, Peru, Puerto Rico, Spain, Uruguay and Venezuela. Many people also speak Spanish in parts of the United States such as New York City, the Southwest, and Southeast.

Un saltarín: A jumping bean is not a bean. It is a larva, a small worm inside a seed. The worm makes the seed wobble. In Spanish, a jumping bean is called **un saltarín.**

You can buy jumping beans online. When you receive yours, give it a Spanish name. Here are some ideas: **Pepito, Paquita, Chuchito, Tito, Chucho, Nachito, Chiquito, Chiquita.**

Be sure to speak to your jumping bean in Spanish!

Frijoles: These are beans that can be dried. **Frijoles** are often dried before they are sold. They are very popular in Mexico. There are many different types: black, white, pink and pinto (mottled).

The preparation of beans varies from one region to another. Is there a section for Mexican or Hispanic foods in your neighborhood supermarket? If so, see how many dried and canned types of **frijoles** you can find.

Mercado: Most cities and villages in Mexico have a market. Markets can be indoors or outdoors. Each vendor has a stall where he or she sells fruit, vegetables, and many other things. Customers are expected to bargain for the price. That means, they don't accept the vendor's price; they offer a lower price. Finally, the vendor and customers settle on a price in between the amounts. The money used in Mexico is the **peso**.

Try bargaining for **un sombrero** with a friend or family member. One person can be the vendor and ask for a high price; the other person can be the customer and ask for a lower price. Finally, agree on a price.

Begin with **Hola, Señor/Señora**.

¿Cuánto cuesta el sombrero? *How much does the hat cost?*

Here are the numbers from 1-10:

1 uno	2 dos	3 tres	4 cuatro	5 cinco
6 seis	7 siete	8 ocho	9 nueve	10 diez

La Piñata:

Piñatas are part of many celebrations in Mexico. They can be made of clay pots or  papier-mâché, and they are colorfully decorated. They come in many shapes: a star **piñata** is used for Christmas. **Piñatas** can be filled with fruit, small toys, or candy.

At the party, the **piñata** is hung high. The players are blindfolded and they take turns trying to break the **piñata** while the others sing and shout hints and words of encouragement.

Have a **piñata** party. You can order a **piñata** on the Internet. Fill it with your favorite **caramelos**.

Encourage the blindfolded player by saying: **¡Dale!**

Hit it! Use Spanish expressions during **la fiesta** such as: **¡Riquísimo! ¡Caramba! ¡Vamos, amigos! ¡Miren! Por favor**.

DALE, DALE, DALE

*Here's **la canción**, the song, that everyone sings while the player tries to break the **piñata**:*

Dale, Dale, Dale	Hit it, hit it, hit it
No pierdas el tino	Don't lose your aim
Porque si lo pierdes	Because if you lose it
Pierdes el camino	You'll lose the way
Ya le diste uno	You already hit once
Ya le diste dos	You already hit twice
Ya le diste tres	You already hit three times
Y tu tiempo se acabó	And your turn is over
Ándale Juana	Hurry up, Juanita
No te dilates	Don't be slow
Con la canasta	With the basket
De los cacahuates	of peanuts
No quiero niquel	I don't want nickel
Ni quiero plata	I don't want silver
Yo lo que quiero	What I want
Es romper la piñata	Is to break the piñata

UNA MÁSCARA *A Mask*

People in Mexico have been making masks for thousands of years. Masks were once used for religious ceremonies. Today, they are worn during festivals and some dances. Masks can be very colorful, and sometimes very scary! The masks can look like people or animals, or a combination. Masks are usually made from wood, clay, papier-mâché, or cardboard, and decorated with precious stones, and lots of other materials.
Let's make **una máscara** and decorate it with **frijoles**. **¡Es fácil!** It's easy!

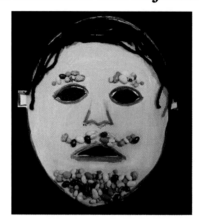

Materials: oaktag of any color, dried beans (**frijoles**), glue, tempera paint and brush (if you want flesh or "peach" or another color), markers, scissors, paper, elastic string, pencil. You may want to use yarn for the hair. Ask your parents to buy colorful dried beans.
The masks and patterns shown look like Mexican masks of men and women.

1. First, make the pattern on paper. Fold the sheet of paper in half, draw a half circle, cut along the line, and then unfold. Ask an adult to mark where your eyes and mouth are, and make a triangle for your nose. Cut out the eyes, mouth, and bottom part of the nose. Make ears or tabs on the sides of the face so that you can attach an elastic string if you want to wear the mask.
2. Cut out the face, put it on a piece of oaktag, and trace around it with a pencil. Ask an adult to help you cut out the openings for the eyes, mouth, and nose on the oaktag. Or, you can paste the template to the oaktag and then do the cutting.
3. If you would like flesh color, paint the mask using tempera paint and a paint-brush and let it dry.
4. Outline the eyes and mouth using markers.
5. Decide how you want to use the beans. For a man, you can create a mustache,

eyebrows, hair, and a beard. For a woman, you can create eyebrows, earrings, and hair. Or, you can put the beans anywhere you choose. Outline the eyebrows, etc., in pencil. Put glue on the places where you are putting the beans. Place or drop the beans while the glue is still wet. Glue yarn for hair, or draw hair with markers if not using yarn or beans.

6. Let the mask dry for a long time. Attach elastic string to the ears or tabs if you want to wear the mask.

7. Put the mask on. **¡Qué bonito!** How nice! How pretty! **¡Me gusta!** I like it!

PATTERN FOR MAN'S MASK

PATTERN FOR WOMAN'S MASK

PALABRAS  Words

These are the words that have been introduced in the book , organized by chapter:

HOLA

adiós	good-bye	**un niño**	a boy
un campo	a field	**una niña**	a girl
cinco	five	**niños**	children
cuatro	four	**no**	no
dos	two	**por favor**	please
frijoles	beans	**¿Qué tal?**	How are you?
gracias	thank you	**sí**	yes
hola	hello	**tres**	three
Me llamo...	My name is...	**tú**	you
muy bien	very good, very well	**uno**	one
		y	and

PANCHITO

amigos	friends	**¡Qué horror!**	How awful!
¡Ay!	Oh! Oh, my!	**¡Qué mono!**	How cute!
¡Bienvenido!	Welcome!	**¿Qué pasa?**	What's the matter?
¡Caramba!	Darn!	**¡Qué sorpresa!**	What a surprise!
caramelos	candy	**riquísimo**	delicious
¿Cómo te llamas?	What's your name?	**un saltarín**	a jumping bean
		(el) señor	Mr.
una fiesta	a party	**(la) señora**	Mrs.
un hombre	a man	**un sombrero**	a hat
hombres	men	**un tomate**	a tomato
Mamá	Mom	**tomates**	tomatoes
un mercado	a market	**¡Vamos !**	Let's go!
¡Miren!	Look! (to two or more people)		
Papá	Dad		

TE TOCA A TI

¡Aquí estoy!	Here I am!	**un libro**	a book
un árbol	a tree	**mal**	bad, poorly
un armario	a closet (often free-standing wardrobe)	**me**	me
		muy bien	very good, very well
así así	so-so	**un pájaro**	a bird
bailo	I dance	**un pastel**	a cake
bien	well	**un pico**	a beak
el campo	the country(side) the field	**un plato**	a dish
		¡Qué miedo!	That's frightening!
canto	I sing	**¿Qué pasó?**	What happened?
una casa	a house	**¡Qué suerte!**	That's lucky!
cogió	he, she, it caught	**un regalo**	a gift
corro	I run	**salto**	I jump
cosas	things	**¡Socorro!**	Help!
¿dónde?	where?	**soltó**	He, she, it let go
¿Dónde está?	Where is...?	**su**	his, her, its
en	in, at, on	**el supermercado**	supermarket
la escuela	the school	**yo**	I
un globo	a balloon		
hay	there is, there are		
el jardín	the garden, yard		

EL RINCÓN CULTURAL, LA MÁSCARA DE FRIJOLES

diez	ten	**¡Qué bonito!**	How pretty/nice!
el español	Spanish	**seis**	six
¡Es fácil!	It's easy!	**siete**	seven
una máscara	a mask		
Me gusta.	I like it.		
nueve	nine		
ocho	eight		

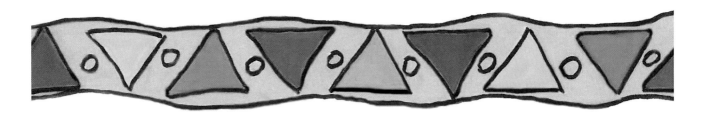

¡MUCHAS GRACIAS!

Many thanks to my friends and colleagues who gave me excellent advice and encouragement:

Denise Abrahamsen-Gallo

Harriet Barnett

Magdalena Barrera de la Peña

Marissa Coulehan

Lisa Giurlanda

Rosemary Haigh

Joan Militscher

María Fernanda Pardo

Louise Terry

Enzina Zaino

Photo of Mexican Jumping Bean: Mihai-Bogdan Lazar, /Dreamstime.com

Musical score for **Dale, Dale, Dale**: Kokila Bennett

Photo of Mexican Market: Jose de Quesada